China's Nuclear Forces: Operations, Training, Doctrine, Command, Control and Campaign Planning

Larry M. Wortzel

The BiblioGov Project is an effort to expand awareness of the public documents and records of the U.S. Government via print publications. In broadening the public understanding of government and its work, an enlightened democracy can grow and prosper. Ranging from historic Congressional Bills to the most recent Budget of the United States Government, the BiblioGov Project spans a wealth of government information. These works are now made available through an environmentally friendly, print-on-demand basis, using only what is necessary to meet the required demands of an interested public. We invite you to learn of the records of the U.S. Government, heightening the knowledge and debate that can lead from such publications.

Included are the following Collections:

Budget of The United States Government
Presidential Documents
United States Code
Education Reports from ERIC
GAO Reports
History of Bills
House Rules and Manual
Public and Private Laws

Code of Federal Regulations
Congressional Documents
Economic Indicators
Federal Register
Government Manuals
House Journal
Privacy act Issuances
Statutes at Large

CHINA'S NUCLEAR FORCES: OPERATIONS, TRAINING, DOCTRINE, COMMAND, CONTROL, AND CAMPAIGN PLANNING

Larry M. Wortzel

May 2007

Visit our website for other free publication downloads
http://www.StrategicStudiesInstitute.army.mil/

To rate this publication click here.

This publication is a work of the U.S. Government as defined in Title 17, United States Code, Section 101. As such, it is in the public domain, and under the provisions of Title 17, United States Code, Section 105, it may not be copyrighted.

*****

The views expressed in this report are those of the author and do not necessarily reflect the official policy or position of the Department of the Army, the Department of Defense, or the U.S. Government. This report is cleared for public release; distribution is unlimited.

*****

The author wants to acknowledge Strategic Analysis and Assessment, Scitor Corporation, which provided support for this research.

*****

Comments pertaining to this report are invited and should be forwarded to: Director, Strategic Studies Institute, U.S. Army War College, 122 Forbes Ave, Carlisle, PA 17013-5244.

*****

All Strategic Studies Institute (SSI) publications are available on the SSI homepage for electronic dissemination. Hard copies of this report also may be ordered from our homepage. SSI's homepage address is: *www.StrategicStudiesInstitute.army.mil*.

*****

The Strategic Studies Institute publishes a monthly e-mail newsletter to update the national security community on the research of our analysts, recent and forthcoming publications, and upcoming conferences sponsored by the Institute. Each newsletter also provides a strategic commentary by one of our research analysts. If you are interested in receiving this newsletter, please subscribe on our homepage at *www.StrategicStudiesInstitute.army.mil/newsletter/*.

ISBN 1-58487-292-6

FOREWORD

A decade ago, many scholars and policy analysts who followed China dismissed the People's Liberation Army (PLA) as an antiquated force that was essentially infantry, fighting with decades-old weapons, poor communications, and World War II era doctrine. China's nuclear forces were also technologically outmoded and fixed to silo or tunnel launch sites. Very little information was available about China's "Second Artillery Corps," as China calls its strategic rocket forces. The United States knew that the PLA maintained a separate corps of rocket troops, but its doctrine and command and control structures remained shrouded in secrecy. Chinese diplomats, political leaders, and security thinkers regularly announced that China would adhere to a "no first use" policy, but very little published military information was available about how China intended to use its missile forces in crisis or war.

Dr. Larry M. Wortzel's monograph sheds new light on the operations, training, and doctrine of the Second Artillery Corps. The PLA is adding modernized mobile missile forces to the older silo-based strategic forces. At the same time, China is experimenting with multiple reentry vehicles, maneuverable reentry vehicles, and other penetration aids or countermeasures on its warheads as measures to respond to potential missile defenses. A nation-wide network of redundant command and control systems is now deployed around China to ensure retaliatory capabilities are available and responsive to the orders of the Chinese Communist Party's Central Military Commission. The PLA has generated new doctrine on how to integrate missile forces into its military campaigns at the operational level of war while still maintaining the strategic nuclear deterrent.

However, there are some worrisome aspects to this modernization. China has mixed nuclear, nuclear-capable, and conventionally armed missiles into its theater (or campaign)-level forces. It has worked to perfect ballistic missiles that can attack moving targets at sea. Moreover, it has integrated submarine-launched ballistic missiles into its nuclear doctrine. Among civilian strategists and military officers, a debate has developed about the viability of China's "no-first-use" pledges in the age of precision weapons and stealth attack. Additionally, the PLA is now publishing more military theoretical studies and doctrine on these changes and how to employ them, providing new information on China's capabilities, organization, and threat perceptions.

We are pleased to present this monograph, which provides new insights into why China's leaders and military thinkers see the United States as a major potential threat to the PLA and China's interests. The monograph also discusses the relationships between conventional and nuclear ballistic units in war fighting doctrine. These are critical matters for the Army and our nation.

DOUGLAS C. LOVELACE, JR.
Director
Strategic Studies Institute

BIOGRAPHICAL SKETCH OF THE AUTHOR

LARRY M. WORTZEL is a leading authority on China and Asia. Dr. Wortzel had a distinguished 32-year military career, retiring as a colonel in 1999. His last military position was as Director of the Strategic Studies Institute of the U.S. Army War College. After retiring from the Army, Wortzel was Asian Studies Center Director and then Vice President for Foreign Policy Studies at The Heritage Foundation, a public policy "think tank" in Washington D.C. He is a commissioner on the congressionally-appointed U.S.-China Economic and Security Review. After 3 years in the United States Marine Corps and some college, Dr. Wortzel began his professional career assessing political and military events in China as a sergeant in the U.S. Army Security Agency in 1970. He gathered communications intelligence on Chinese military activities in Laos and Vietnam during the Vietnam War. After Infantry Officer Candidate School, Ranger, and Airborne training he was an infantry officer for 4 years. He moved back into military intelligence in 1977. He has traveled regularly to China since 1979. He served two tours of duty as a military attaché at the American Embassy in China. Dr. Wortzel's books include *Class in China; China's Military Modernization; The Chinese Armed Forces in the 21st Century*; and *Dictionary of Contemporary Chinese Military History*. A graduate of the Armed Forces Staff College and the U.S. Army War College, Dr. Wortzel earned his B.A. from Columbus College, Georgia, and his M.A. and Ph.D. from the University of Hawaii.

SUMMARY

The major insights in this monograph come from exploiting sections of a doctrinal text published for People's Liberation Army (PLA) institutions of higher military education by the Chinese National Defense University, *A Guide to the Study of Campaign Theory (Zhanyi Lilun Xuexi Zhinan)*. This book is an unclassified "study guide" for PLA officers on how to understand and apply doctrine in a restricted PLA book on campaign doctrine in warfare, *The Science of Campaigns*. Other recent books by PLA or Chinese government controlled publishing houses validate the insights in the monograph and demonstrate how the PLA is going about achieving its vision for modern war fighting.

These materials provide new insights into China's Second Artillery Corps, the "Strategic Rocket Forces." Chinese strategists believe that China must be prepared to fight in, and if necessary, control space; which explains the 2006 laser attack on a U.S. satellite from China and the 2007 anti-satellite missile test by the Chinese. PLA officers also believe that U.S. satellite reconnaissance from space could constitute a threat to China's nuclear deterrent.

China's leaders and military thinkers see the United States as a major potential threat to the PLA and China's interests primarily because of American military capabilities, but also because of U.S. security relationships in Asia. To respond to these perceived threats, China's military thinkers are examining the relationships between conventional and nuclear ballistic missile units in war and developing new doctrine for missile employment. There are explicit discussions in PLA military literature and scientific journals on how to use ballistic missiles to attack deployed U.S. naval battle groups, particularly aircraft carriers. Indeed, the Second Artillery Corps is developing a new class of maneuvering reentry vehicles with this mission in mind. In addition, there is also more open information revealed in these documents about frontal and national-level command and control of missile units.

The targets suggested for theater warfare and conventional guided missile campaigns at the operational level of war are designed to achieve battlefield effects that will destroy an enemy's ability to wage war effectively. Secondarily, the targets selected would disrupt the enemy's economy, reconstitution and resupply capabilities:
- Enemy political centers;
- Economic centers;
- Major enemy military bases and depots;
- Enemy command centers;
- Enemy communications and transportation networks; and,
- Major troop concentrations.

China's strategic intercontinental ballistic missile force remains primarily retaliatory in nature. The PLA may employ theater and shorter-range ballistic missiles, however, as elements of a surprise attack or to preempt an enemy attack. PLA military thinkers recognize that long-range precision strike by conventional weapons is now an integral part of U.S. military doctrine. They fear that a conventional attack on China's strategic missile forces could render China vulnerable and leave it without a deterrent. This has led to a debate in China among civilian strategic thinkers and military leaders on the viability of the announced "no-first-use" policy on nuclear weapons. Some strategists advocate departing from the "no-first-use" policy and responding to conventional attacks on strategic forces with nuclear missiles.

The objectives for nuclear campaign planning are ambiguous enough to leave open the question of preemptive action by the PLA. According to *A Guide to the Study of Campaign Theory,* a major objective of Chinese nuclear planning is to "alter enemy intentions by causing the enemy's will [to engage in war] to waver." Preemption, therefore, would be a viable action that is consistent with the PLA's history of "self-defensive counterattacks."

The PLA leadership has prioritized the objectives of nuclear counterattack campaigns as follows:
- Cause the will of the enemy (and the populace) to waver;
- Destroy the enemy's command and control system;[1]
- Delay the enemy's war (or combat) operations;
- Reduce the enemy's force generation and war-making potential; and,
- Degrade the enemy's ability to win a nuclear war.

The decision by Beijing to put nuclear and conventional warheads on the same classes of ballistic missiles and colocate them near each other in firing units of the Second Artillery Corps also increases the risk of accidental nuclear conflict. A critical factor in any American decision will be the capabilities of American space-based sensor systems. Accurate sensors may be able to determine whether China launched a conventional or nuclear-tipped missile, and such a determination could prevent immediate escalation of a crisis or conflict.

These are serious matters for the American armed forces. China's nuclear forces are evolving and the way they are used is under debate. The way that the PLA handles its commitment to dominating space and its commitment to being capable of attacking American command, control, communication, computers, intelligence, surveillance, and reconnaissance (C4ISR) systems affects strategic warning, missile defenses, and command and control. For the Army, with the responsibility to defend the United States against missile attack, it means that watching the evolution of this debate in China is critical to success.

ENDNOTE

1. Xin Qin reinforces this, writing that "one must attack the C4ISR network that supports the command and control system of an enemy, particularly one that is fighting a war on external lines [in other words, an enemy fighting a power projection war]." Xin, *Xinxihua Shidai de Zhanzheng* (*Warfare in the Information Age*), Beijing: National Defense University Press, 2000, p. 90.

CHINA'S NUCLEAR FORCES: OPERATIONS, TRAINING, DOCTRINE, COMMAND, CONTROL, AND CAMPAIGN PLANNING

Introduction.

This monograph analyzes several recent Chinese language books published by the People's Liberation Army (PLA) for information about China's Second Artillery Corps, their "Strategic Rocket Forces." These materials provide new insights into why China's leaders and military thinkers see the United States as a major potential threat to the PLA and China's interests. The materials also discuss the relationships they see between conventional and nuclear ballistic missile units in war fighting doctrine. There are explicit discussions of how to use missiles to attack deployed United States naval forces. There are important discussions of how the control of space relates to China's nuclear deterrence. There is also more open information revealed in these documents about frontal and national-level command and control of missile units. Finally, the materials provide insights into the evolving debate in China between civilian strategic thinkers and military leaders on the viability of an announced "no-first-use" policy on nuclear weapons.

The major insights in this monograph come from exploiting sections of a doctrinal text published for PLA institutions of higher military education by the Chinese National Defense University, *A Guide to the Study of Campaign Theory*.[1] This book is an unclassified "study guide" for PLA officers on how to understand and apply doctrine in a restricted PLA book on campaign doctrine in warfare, *The Science of Campaigns*.[2] Other recent books by PLA or Chinese government controlled publishing houses validate the insights in the paper and demonstrate how the PLA is going about achieving its vision for modern war fighting. These include *On Strategic Command and Control*, published by Military Science Press in 2002; and *Warfare in the Information Age*, published by National Defense University Press in 2000.

To assist the PLA in its goal of attacking deployed aircraft carrier battle groups, two PLA Air Force (PLAAF) authors, Sun Yiming and Yang Liping, have built a virtual roadmap for attacking joint U.S. data control systems and military communications. They have carefully consulted dozens of corporate web sites and military tactical data link operator guides, as well as North Atlantic Treaty Organization (NATO) and U.S. military tactical and technical manuals, to produce a virtual guidebook for electronic warfare and jamming to disrupt critical U.S. cooperative target engagement and command, control, communications, computers, and intelligence, surveillance and reconnaissance (C4ISR) data links: *Tactical Data Links in Information Warfare*.[3]

On the debate over China's "no-first-use" policy among the academic community, younger PLA authors, and the older generation of PLA leaders, this paper relies on interviews with strategists and PLA academics in 2006, and the book, *International Politics and China*, published by Peking University Press in 2005. The PLA's traditional approach to the subject is set forth in a doctrinal text, *China's National Defense and World Military Affairs*, endorsed by General Zhang Wannian, who was chief of the General Staff Department of the PLA at the time it was published.[4]

However, China's traditional approach of "no-first-use" of nuclear weapons is under challenge by the new generation of strategists. Finally, the paper explores ways that the PLA's concept of "active defense" relates to nuclear doctrine.

The United States as the Greatest Potential Threat.

One of the key insights from these documents is that China now identifies the United States as its main potential enemy, although in some materials, the references to the United States are indirect. This is an important change in China's strategic literature because in the past, Russia (the Soviet Union) was also identified as a principal threat to China. Now the United States stands alone.

In part, this is because senior PLA leaders and military strategists consider the United States to be the most advanced military force on which to base their own military development. They also see the United States as the most advanced and likely potential enemy against which they may need to employ ballistic and cruise missiles or counter advanced C4ISR technologies.

According to the monthly Hong Kong magazine, *Cheng Ming*, after a large-scale Second Artillery exercise, Vice Chairman of the Central Military Commission (CMC) General Guo Boxiong addressed the participants to discuss the posture the PLA should maintain toward the United States. General Guo told the exercise participants, "China must strive to increase the capabilities of its strategic nuclear weapons if it wants to stand firm against the United States, which routinely treats China as an enemy in its strategic planning."[5]

In the view of many in the PLA, the military power of the United States, the potential to use that power to coerce or dominate China, and the ability to threaten China's pursuit of its own interests, presents a latent threat to China. Additionally, China's own threats against democratic Taiwan, and the fact that PLA leaders believe that the United States is likely to come to Taiwan's assistance in the event of Chinese aggression in the Taiwan Strait, magnifies the threat that PLA officers perceive from the United States. This perceived threat drives the PLA to follow U.S. military developments more carefully than those of other nations and to be prepared to counter American forces.

Over the past decade, authors at the PLA National Defense University have singled out the United States as the world's greatest political, military, and economic power, and the only such power that can act on a global scale. An assessment of the U.S. nuclear posture in the post-Cold War period said: "The goal of America's new military strategy after the collapse of the Soviet Union is to maintain the U.S. position as a world superpower and maintain America's position as a world leader. The maintenance of a strong nuclear deterrent by the United States is an important tool for the United States."[6]

Today, PLA literature often refers to "great powers" with the ability to coerce other countries because of their nuclear and military capabilities, or PLA writers refer to "hegemonic powers" that threaten peace. The former phrasing, "great powers with the ability to coerce other countries," is an indirect reference to both Russia and the United States. The latter formulation, however, "hegemonic powers that threaten peace," is shorthand for the United States.

Major General Wang Baocun of the PLA Academy of Military Science summarized the view of the United States this way:

> The new military transformation has led to the rise of a United States possessed of overwhelmingly dominant military might. The United States is also an arrogant country with strong ambitions for hegemonism. The United States will take advantage of its absolute superiority in supreme military might in order to pursue power politics and hegemonism, seek to maintain its position as the world's only superpower, and slow down the process of mulitpolarization for the world's strategic structure.[7]

Such a view is fueling the PLA's efforts to build a modern, information-based, digitized military force. PLA thinkers believe that the missiles in the Second Artillery Corps (Strategic Rocket Forces) are a "trump card" that, when combined with information warfare, will help the PLA to win a war against a more advanced military.[8] Indeed, even if the PLA did not envision seeking a direct confrontation with the United States, the awareness that the two countries could clash in the event of a Chinese attack on Taiwan is enough to drive PLA modernization.

General Zhang Wannian, then chief of the General Staff Department of the PLA, has argued that "modern limited warfare under high technology conditions is conducted under a cloud of a threat of becoming a nuclear war, and this cloud or shadow of nuclear war will limit the scope of warfare."[9] He suggests that the "forces of hegemony in the world will use nuclear weapons to dominate other nations," thus China must have nuclear capabilities. In this context, the reference to "forces of hegemony" is a part of Zhang's comments on the First Gulf War and is shorthand for the United States. It is a clear reference to the United States as a potential enemy. Moreover, Zhang's book contains other indirect references to the United States as a potential enemy when he suggests that China's nuclear weapons can be used to "deter moves to split the sovereign state," a reference to Taiwan.[10] Finally, Zhang notes that the conduct of "bloody actual combat" (during conventional war), in itself, is a deterrent measure, and the more destructive the actual combat in which a nation engages, the greater the likelihood of effective deterrence.[11]

A good example of an indirect statement of perceptions of the threat posed to China by the United States is Xia Liping's explanation of the logic behind China's strategy of "Active Defense." Xia is a reserve senior colonel in the PLA affiliated with the Shanghai Institute for International Studies and Fudan University. He set forth the concepts behind the "active defense" strategy for the Chinese Communist Party audience in a periodical from the Central Communist Party School. Xia tells the reader that the CMC studied and considered the conduct of the Gulf War (1990-91) and in 1993 decided on a strategy of "active defense" to meet the demand of the "world's new revolution in military affairs (RMA), as well as other factors threatening China's security."[12] The reference to the Gulf War and the RMA are intellectual shorthand for the United States. However, the concept of "active defense" is not new in Chinese military thinking and is embedded in the military doctrines espoused by Mao Zedong.

The view that the United States has greater potential than other nations to threaten China is consistent with that in a book by one of the most respected PLA strategists and leaders, Lieutenant General Li Jijun,

Thinking about Military Strategy. Li commanded a Group Army in Manchuria and was responsible for the ground warfare experiment that validated combined arms group armies in the PLA. Later he was the director of Deng Xiaoping's military office. In retirement, he teaches advanced military theory courses at the PLA Academy of Military Science and at Beijing University. Originally published in 1996, Li's book was revised and republished twice by the Academy of Military Science, most recently in 2002.

In his evaluation of contemporary world security threats, Li Jijun concludes that the major problem facing China is "large countries" that create "threat theories, including the countries that espouse the 'China threat theory'."[13] Of course, this is a clear, albeit indirect, reference to the United States as the nation with the most capability to threaten China because of its policies, its military power, and its alliances.[14]

Li says,

> . . . like England (in the Napoleonic age), the U.S. is the world's strongest power; the United States has the greatest number of international interests and "colonial" [like] relationships; U.S. military power is dispersed widely throughout the world; the wide range of interests and military deployments mean that U.S. forces are over-committed and stretched thin; and there is a great need to work with allies and coalition partners to achieve security goals.[15]

Concern over the United States and its military power is not limited to the PLA. One prominent civilian scholar, Yan Xuetong, believes that the United States is "the dominant world military power for a 10 to 20-year period, and in that period is the only threat to China."[16] Yan spent a decade as a staff member of the China Institute for Contemporary International

Relations, a government institute related to the Ministry of State Security. Today he is a professor at Tsinghua University and is still summoned to brief senior military and civilian officials of the government and the Chinese Communist Party.

China's most recent *White Paper on National Defense*, issued on December 29, 2006, also warns "the United States is accelerating is realignment of military deployment to enhance its military capability in the Asia-Pacific region."[17] The White Paper further expresses concern that "the United States and Japan are strengthening their military alliance in pursuit of operational integration" . . . while Japan's military posture is "becoming more external-oriented."

Although there is passing discussion of the nuclear forces of Russia and India in these publications, the authors do not classify them as major strategic threats to China. The same is true of Japan. The authors acknowledge Japan as a military power, but Chinese strategists seem to think that Japan's populace remains satisfied by the U.S. strategic nuclear umbrella.

Guided Missiles in Conventional War Campaigns.

New doctrine for the employment of missiles in warfare emphasizes the value of strategic missiles as a form of offset attack, particularly in China's military strategy of the "active defense." The "active defense" concept holds that warfare is a "holistic entity that includes offensive as well as defensive action."[18] In a strategic defense, according to PLA doctrine, offensive action still carries the war to the enemy; thus, counterattack is one form of offensive action within a general strategic defense.[19] PLA doctrine holds that "active defense strategy does not acknowledge the difference . . . between offense and defense, . . . and sudden 'first strikes' in campaigns or battles as well as 'counterattacks in self defense' into enemy territory are part of the doctrine."[20] Some Chinese believe that the concept of "active defense" permits the conduct of preemptive attacks.[21]

The doctrine in *A Guidebook to the Study of Campaign Theory* gives specific guidance for the conduct of conventional guided missile campaigns.[22] According to this text, the Second Artillery force has subordinate to the headquarters a "conventional guided missile campaign army group."[23] The army group must be "continuously prepared for a rapid response," which indicates a series of prepared war plans are maintained within the conventional force. The doctrine for conventional guided missile forces calls for the use of a "small amount of force as a deterrent against attack."[24]

The targets suggested for conventional guided missile campaigns are designed to achieve battlefield effects that will destroy an enemy's ability to wage war effectively. In addition, the targets selected would disrupt the enemy's economy, reconstitution and resupply capabilities:
- Enemy political centers;
- Economic centers;
- Major enemy military bases and depots;
- Enemy command centers;
- Enemy communications and transportation networks; and,
- Major troop concentrations.[25]

The Second Artillery Conventional Guided Missile Campaign Army Group operates under the direct leadership of the CMC. However, conventional battlefield missiles are assigned to military regions or war fronts and operate under the control of the regional or frontal commander.[26]

There are regular references to the need to "mass (or concentrate) fires" against critical targets. General Zhang Wannian reminds the PLA in one text "from the standpoint of firepower, air bombardment, artillery, and guided missiles must be massed for the greatest long-range destructive and killing effect."[27] Xin Qin makes the same point several times in his book, *Information Age Warfare*. He emphasizes that "to ensure a decisive attack against a target, guided missiles (ballistic or cruise missiles) must be massed against their objective."[28] He notes that the effective use of conventional ballistic missiles can "win a war without engagement [i.e., without employing one's own troops in direct combat] if their offensive fires are concentrated effectively."[29] He is very critical of Iraq in the First Gulf War for failing to concentrate missile fires effectively against decisive troop targets.[30]

This approach to warfare of employing concentrated ballistic and cruise missile fires clearly informs the PLA's strategy against Taiwan, where the short-range ballistic missile build-up has reached about 800. In addition, the PLA has developed new classes of land attack cruise missiles which could be used against Taiwan. It is also likely that if the PLA decides to use conventional ballistic or cruise missiles in naval warfare, they will concentrate missile fire against key naval formations.

There also is an identifiable logic chain of battlefield lessons-learned and analysis that led the PLA to its current doctrine. Strategists and senior generals in the PLA were highly critical of Iraq's performance in the aftermath of the First Gulf War. The PLA's studies from the First Gulf War informed the campaign doctrine and guidance on the use of missiles today in texts like *A Guide to the Study of Campaign Theory*.[31]

To illustrate how these lessons affect military thought today, in *Information Age Warfare,* Xin Qin, a PLA staff officer, argues that Iraq never used its ballistic missiles effectively.[32] Iraqi missile forces failed by not gathering the necessary intelligence of American and allied assembly areas, and they compounded that failure by not taking the initiative to attack them. He argues for the massing of fires against critical targets by ballistic missile forces. Xin believes that if Iraq had massed its "guided missile strength against the weaker coalition forces before they left training and assembly areas, they [those forces] could have been destroyed before they moved into combat formations and attack positions."[33]

This has been the consistent view in the PLA for over a decade. General Zhang Zhen, then vice chairman of the CMC, endorsed it in *Guided Missile Combat and High Technology Wars.* In that book, the authors point out that "the combat power of missiles is very high, but they must be used on enemy troop concentrations, important bases or facilities, or other command and control nerve centers in a *sudden attack by concentrated fires.*"[34] They go on to point out, "Iraq fired 81 *Scud* missiles but failed to produce serious casualties or to affect battlefield operations in a significant way. Therefore, Iraq failed to take advantage of either the killing power of missiles or their psychological effect on operations."[35] The authors summarized their study with the lesson that "missiles must be massed on critical targets, [and] must be accurate" to be effective in war.[36]

With respect to Japan, the lessons that PLA planners took from the Gulf Wars mean that in the future, defense planners in the United States and Japan must watch for a parallel buildup of DF-21s.[37] The PLA will need more of these mobile, medium-range missiles to develop a parallel level of threat against Japan and Okinawa and the capability to carry out that threat, should it be necessary to do so in the future.

Attacking Deployed Carrier Battle Groups.

The PLA seems to believe it is coming close to achieving a goal stated a decade ago—being able to attack a deployed U.S. aircraft carrier battle group with ballistic missiles. It is not clear, however, if the intent is to use conventional warheads or to conduct a nuclear attack. Nor is it clear if, in the event of a nuclear attack, the carrier battle group would be targeted directly or if a high altitude burst would be used to ensure that only electro-magnetic pulse effects are felt, destroying U.S. command, control, and sensor systems and clearing the way for a conventional attack.

One PLA Academy of Military Science researcher expressed the view that to engage in modern war, the PLA must be able to "attack the enemy's knowledge systems and such high value targets as communications, carrier battle groups, and aviation warfare units."[38] According to an officer from the Navy Command Academy who addressed a PLA-wide conference on missile warfare, "the Second Artillery is the major factor in successfully attacking an enemy naval battle group."[39] To accomplish such an attack, this officer said:

> The PLA must use all of its electronic warfare and reconnaissance assets properly, must neutralize enemy anti-missile systems and missile sensor systems, and should use electronic jamming on the enemy fleet. The PLA can then attack the enemy fleet or naval bases with

a combination of explosive, anti-radiation and fake warheads to deceive enemy radar and sensor systems and defeat a deployed battle group or one in port.[40]

For some time American naval officers have dismissed this capability as beyond the grasp of the PLA. American officers believe that China does not have the space sensor systems, relay satellites, and maneuvering warheads required to execute such an attack. However, PLA officers seem convinced that using ballistic missiles to attack naval battle groups is a viable concept, and they are working to develop the necessary systems to do so.

For a military force like the PLA, without a naval air arm with a long reach, with a very limited aerial refueling capability, and with older air platforms, using ballistic missiles for this purpose makes sense. Three PLA officers from the Second Artillery Command Academy advance the idea that "guided missile forces are the trump card *(sa shou jian)* in achieving victory in limited high technology war."[41] The keys to achieving such capabilities, in the argument of other PLA officers, lie in three areas: the use of countermeasures, the ability to achieve precision targeting, and the use of space platforms to support the effort.[42]

Two officers from the Second Artillery Engineering College have studied how to modify a mobile trajectory for warhead reentry into the atmosphere to determine the effective range for attacking an enemy aircraft carrier with ballistic missiles.[43] They conclude that providing terminal guidance will allow up to 100 kilometers of maneuverability for a warhead during terminal attack. They believe that a carrier "cannot effectively escape an attack within a short period of time."[44]

Simulations to predict how the final attack ranges for maneuvering targets at sea will affect maneuvering reentry vehicles are also part of the research agenda for Second Artillery engineering officers.⁴⁵ They have concluded that because a carrier battle group can project force out to about 2,500 kilometers, the PLA must reduce its missile warhead circular error probable to attack maneuvering targets at sea outside the carrier's strike range.

Nuclear Counterattack Campaigns.

Long-standing published military doctrine, statements by senior leaders, and the force preservation measures undertaken by the PLA all support the conclusion that the Second Artillery's strategic mission is principally to be a deterrent and retaliatory force. The accounts of tunneling by Second Artillery engineers in military press and journals, as well as command and control measures, all reinforce this conclusion. However, there is a debate going on in China about the utility of "no-first-use" declarations. Specifically, military thinkers in China are discussing how to respond to conventional attacks on strategic systems and how to respond to intelligence warning of imminent strategic attack. The latter debate keeps open the question of "preemptive counterattacks," something China has done in conventional war.

There are several large and unanswered questions that this section of the paper attempts to address. First, would the PLA execute a "preemptive nuclear counterattack" if it believed an adversary was about to attack China? One part of the PLA doctrine says, "Advance warning may come to the Second Artillery before an attack if there is notice that the enemy may use nuclear weapons on any scale."⁴⁶ This implies that the PLA might order a launch to preempt an enemy surprise attack.⁴⁷ Such a preemptive attack is consistent with the concept of the "active defense," which permits sudden, surprise attacks into enemy territory and "self-defensive counterattacks."⁴⁸ Moreover, as China achieves improved levels of sophistication in space surveillance, tracking, and relay, will judgments about the propriety of "preemptive nuclear counterattack" change?

Space is the area above 100,000 meters from sea level. There are clear indications in PLA doctrine that China wants the capacity to control space and intends to control space immediately above its own territory. One PLA officer has written "in peacetime or wartime, enemy reconnaissance satellites are the greatest threat to guided missile forces."⁴⁹ In addition, Chinese military theorists are convinced that for the security of China's nuclear forces, the PLA needs anti-satellite countermeasures to stop an enemy's ability to use satellite surveillance against the Second Artillery Corps. According to one officer writing in the journal, *China Military Science*, "in order to assure the nation's space security, it is necessary to develop defensive mechanisms; this requires work in the electro-magnetic spectrum as well as firepower-based defenses."⁵⁰

Taken together, these considerations undermine the strength of China's "no-first-use" guarantees. Even the language in the 2006 *National Defense White Paper* is somewhat ambiguous. The White Paper declares "China remains firmly committed to the policy of no first use of nuclear weapons at any time and under any circumstances." However, the next sentence of the White Paper tells the reader "it unconditionally undertakes a pledge not to use or threaten to use nuclear weapons against non-nuclear weapon states or nuclear-weapon-free zones. . . ." One does not need to be an international lawyer or grammarian to understand that a "firm commitment to policy" is not as strong a position as an "unconditional" pledge.

On January 11, 2007, China destroyed one of its own weather satellites with a kinetic kill vehicle launched on a Chinese missile. Earlier, in August 2006, a Chinese ground-based laser blinded a U.S. reconnaissance satellite over China.[51] Thus, Beijing has demonstrated an anti-satellite capability and has justified such actions in its own military doctrine.

Notwithstanding the debate about China's "no-first-use" policy, based on contemporary periodical articles and military books, current doctrine is to ensure that sufficient strategic missile forces survive a nuclear attack for 3 to 5 days. After this period, Second Artillery doctrine apparently calls for them to emerge, deploy and retaliate in a nuclear counterattack.

The Second Artillery has three main missions: deterrence, supporting conventional war with ballistic missile attacks, and nuclear counterattack.[52] With regard to strategic systems, the PLA focus is "executing nuclear counterattack campaigns."[53] The PLA's plans for nuclear counterattack campaigns are to "deter and prevent the enemy from using nuclear weapons against China" or to "execute a counterattack with nuclear and precision conventional weapons."[54] The PLA's published doctrine, as well as statements by members of the leadership, emphasize that China intends to maintain a survivable nuclear force that can ride out any nuclear attack, and then inflict a counterattack on the enemy.[55]

At the strategic level, *A Guide to the Study of Campaign Theory* lays out the characteristics of a nuclear counterattack campaign. The Second Artillery will use long-range nuclear weapons to destroy strategic targets several thousands of kilometers away.[56] Campaign planners envision carrying out a nuclear attack "only after the enemy carries out a nuclear surprise attack," requiring a force that can absorb and survive an enemy nuclear attack.[57] The existing nuclear counterattack campaign plans involve missile units of the Second Artillery, supplemented by forces of the PLA Navy (PLAN) and/or PLAAF. Moreover, now that the PLA has developed longer-range, nuclear capable cruise missiles, these campaign plans call for the Navy to use submarine launched ballistic or cruise missiles.[58] The PLAAF could attack with nuclear cruise missiles or bombs.

In planning nuclear counterattack campaigns, the PLA gives primacy to the Second Artillery. Doctrine says, "If it is a joint or combined nuclear counterattack campaign plan, the Second Artillery will be the main component combined with naval nuclear submarines and air bombardment with nuclear weapons."[59]

China's nuclear retaliatory plans require that the Second Artillery maintain a force sufficient to "threaten the opponent by striking his cities," and employ a strike force of "moderate intensity" that is "sufficient and effective" to cause the enemy to incur "a certain extent of unbearable destruction."[60] Thus, the size and composition of any nuclear counterattack is a function of a nuclear net assessment by Chinese political and military leaders. It is a function of what they assess as the level of damage the American public, and its leaders, would find "unbearable."

The objectives for nuclear campaign planning are also ambiguous enough to leave open the question of preemptive action by the PLA. According to *A Guide to the Study of Campaign Theory*, major objective of a nuclear counterattack campaign is to "alter enemy intentions by causing the enemy's will [to engage in war] to waver."[61] Preemption, therefore, would be a viable action that is consistent with the PLA's history of "self-defensive counterattacks."[62]

The PLA leadership has prioritized the objectives of nuclear counterattack campaigns. These are:
- Cause the will of the enemy (and the populace) to waver;
- Destroy the enemy's command and control system;[63]
- Delay the enemy's war (or combat) operations;
- Reduce the enemy's force generation and war-making potential; and,
- Degrade the enemy's ability to win a nuclear war.[64]

Generally, the targeting guidance to accomplish these objectives is also set forth in *A Guide to the Study of Campaign Theory*. The prioritized major targets for nuclear missile forces are:
- "Enemy political and economic centers, especially important urban areas, with a goal of creating great shock in the enemy population's spirit and destroying their will to wage war;
- Destroy the critical infrastructure of the enemy to weaken the enemy's capacity for war (examples for targets are petroleum refining, storage and shipping links; electric power generation and transmission lines; and major heavy industry);
- Enemy transportation networks;
- Major military targets such as air force and navy staging areas and bases to degrade the ability of these services to wage war; and,
- Major deployed military forces."[65]

Survive a Nuclear Attack: Then Retaliate.

The guiding motto for the Second Artillery is "strictly protect counterattack capability and concentrate [nuclear] fires to inflict the most damage in the counterattack."[66] They emphasize that the Second Artillery's strategic warning system is closely tied to the General Staff Department and that the Second Artillery must continually keep up an estimate of whether the enemy will use other forms of weapons of mass destruction (WMD).[67]

According to members of a Chinese delegation at a 2005 strategic dialogue organized by the Defense Threat Reduction Agency, the goals of China's nuclear policy are to maintain a retaliatory force of minimum deterrent value and to hold enemy populations at risk.[68] China's seeks to ensure reliable force with adequate delivery systems that can survive a foreign attack and maintains a "counter-value force" that requires modernization.[69]

The CMC and its General Staff Department maintains light strategic forces.[70] The Second Artillery ensures that its communications with firing units are secure and responsive to the Party political leadership.[71] Moreover, even in the computer age, PLA thinkers prefer to rely on soldiers "at the trigger" over automated command and firing systems.[72]

To maintain the force at high levels of readiness, strategic rocket force commanders gather intelligence, maintain a system for indications and warning of attack, and focus on force survivability.

Classes of Readiness for the Second Artillery.

According to *A Guidebook to the Study of Campaign Theory*, the Second Artillery must "continually focus on discovering the enemy's attempts at attack, its times of attack, and must always conduct defensive exercises and preparations."[73] PLA doctrine requires that the Second Artillery "operate and coordinate with air, ground and other defensive organizations under the direction of the CMC to implement a nuclear counterattack campaign."[74]

The Second Artillery has a system of three classes of readiness to which its units must adhere.[75] Under normal conditions, the firing units are at "Third Class" status. In this status, forces train, conduct exercises and conduct normal maintenance. If the CMC receives some warning that the enemy may use nuclear weapons, the CMC directs units to raise their readiness levels to "Second Class" warning status. At this status, units must prepare to move to firing positions or may actually deploy to firing positions, many of which can be tunnels or prepared underground, protected positions. The highest readiness status is "First Class Warning." At "First Class Warning" status, missile forces are fully ready to fire and are either deployed or in combat positions and with their support elements, warheads and fuel, waiting for a launch order.[76]

When firing units actually move to firing positions, the individual unit commanders are responsible for the security of their own prime movers and must conduct a check of the firing status of each missile and the warheads. They must report this status to the headquarters.[77] After firing their missiles, they will disperse and get the results of a post-firing reconnaissance and new intelligence.[78]

Combat orders must come through special command department channels of the Second Artillery or General Staff Department, but only the CMC can send a launch order.[79] The combat order will give the current friendly and enemy situation, the status of the war and a determination on the use of nuclear force, the combat objectives for an attack, and the limits of an attack.[80] The actual firing order will contain the time limits for each unit to fire and instructions for post-firing movement and disposition.[81]

Support for "Guaranteed Survivability and Strike."

The concept of a "guaranteed strike" is fundamental to PLA Second Artillery doctrine. This means that strategic rocket forces must be able to ride out a nuclear attack and emerge later to conduct their counterstrike. To accomplish this, the Second Artillery maintains its own support infrastructure including maintenance, supply and food services, engineers, and road and rail transport.

In a Second Artillery nuclear war simulations exercise reported by China's *Xinhua* news service, China stayed with its "no-first-use" policy and absorbed a nuclear strike. After the strike, the exercise scenario required that the Second Artillery forces stay in protected underground areas for as long as several days before emerging to conduct a retaliatory "nuclear counterattack."[82]

An article in *Beijing Huojianbing Bao (Rocket Troops Daily)*, the Second Artillery's newspaper, provides insight into the tactic of absorbing a strike, waiting a fixed period of time, and then emerging for a "nuclear counterstrike." According to two Second Artillery authors, a 2004 nuclear counterattack exercise had to be stopped in its third day because the troops involved in the exercise developed vomiting and diarrhea from a spoiled food supply.[83] The Second Artillery's Logistics Department adjusted the food supply in future exercises, allowing soldiers to conduct the exercise under "sealed" conditions and extended the safety of the combat food supply. This assured that the Second Artillery could remain underground long enough to emerge safely and conduct a retaliatory strike.

In addition to the PLA Second Artillery Corps engineering and construction units for tunneling and the construction of roads, there is a transportation support infrastructure integral to the organization. An article in *Huojianbing Bao* discusses the Second Artillery rail transport system. A mobile system moved what was termed a "national treasure" by a "rail transportation battalion of a special transportation regiment."[84] Another article in the same paper documents the importance of mobile missiles and mobility training. Rapid mobility is a way to "improve survivability and nuclear counterdeterrence."[85] There also is a continuous program to upgrade and improve missile position design inside the Second Artillery. The objectives of this program are to ensure that missiles are positioned in a way to avoid foreign reconnaissance, take advantage of the geography and environment, and have the maximum possible protection against foreign attack.[86]

The objectives of these integrated support systems are to meet the Second Artillery's "guiding principles for nuclear counterattack campaign strategy." To restate these principles, the guiding motto for the Second Artillery is "strictly protect counterattack capability and concentrate [nuclear] fires to inflict the most damage in the counterattack".[87] To meet the first requirement in this motto, protect and preserve the force, the Second Artillery is to:
- Defend against the enemy's precision weapons attack;
- Defend against enemy air raids;

- Defend against enemy Special Operations Forces attacking China's nuclear forces;
- Organize to respond to sudden surprise attacks; and,
- Organize to restore China's nuclear warfighting capability rapidly.[88]

To meet the second requirement in the motto, "guarantee or safeguard the survivability of the nuclear response system to counterattack," Second Artillery doctrine requires its forces to:
- Protect the nuclear counterattack campaign plan;
- Conduct advanced preparations for a campaign;
- Ensure the timely reliability of the system;
- Be prepared for a rapid response;
- Ensure response plans are complete and comprehensive;
- Guarantee the survivability of the counter attack force; and,
- Conduct comprehensive coordination with other headquarters and commands.[89]

Nuclear Command and Control.

Second Artillery Corps doctrine requires "comprehensive coordination with other headquarters and commands." In order to maintain that level of communication throughout the force, command and control for missile forces is highly centralized, redundant, and networked.[90] Two PLA officers writing in the book *Missile Combat in High Technology Warfare* describe Second Artillery command and control this way: "The nodes in a ballistic missile command

and control network are 1) the commander in chief (*tongshuaibu*), 2) the command organizations of the military departments, 3) the missile bases, and 4) the firing units."[91] Furthermore, they say, "especially where it concerns strategic missiles, the ability of the commander in chief [this can also be translated as "supreme command authority"] to control firing orders must be executed quickly, and firing orders must be encrypted (encoded)."[92] Finally, PLA manuals specify, "the war positions of the Second Artillery are established by the supreme command authority (*tongshuaibu*) in peacetime and are dispersed over a wide area for strategic reasons."[93]

In a text published by the PLA National Defense University, Wang Zhongquan provides a sophisticated analysis of the U.S. strategic warning and nuclear command and control system. Wang bases his analysis on an extensive review of published American literature, but there is no discussion in the text of the dangers or utility of attacking, or disrupting the command and control system. Nor is there a discussion of the advisability of blinding the strategic warning system. The text is a catalogue of the two systems that could support offensive efforts by the PLA, or, alternatively, one can read it as an example for the PLA of how to structure effective warning and command and control systems.[94]

PLA texts emphasize that the Second Artillery's strategic warning system is closely tied to the General Staff Department and that the Second Artillery must continually keep up an estimate of whether the enemy will use other forms of weapons of mass destruction.[95] The use of the term *tongshuaibu* in this context is uncommon, but not unheard of, in explanations of Chinese command and control systems. *Tongshuai* can mean supreme commander or commander in chief. The Nationalist forces (Kuomintang, or KMT) used the term to refer to a couple of major frontal headquarters during the civil war. In the *Huaihai* Campaign, for instance, in 1949, the KMT combat headquarters for the campaign was called the *Tongshuaibu*. PLA military histories also refer to Eisenhower's headquarters for Overlord and the Supreme Headquarters, Allied Powers Europe as the *tongshuaibu*. Clearly, this use is meant to designate a higher-level command authority than the General Staff Department Operations Department.

On the 40th anniversary of the founding of the Second Artillery, Hu Jintao spoke to an assemblage of people that included Xiang Shouzhi, first commander of the organization, and a number of previous leaders. Hu was present in the combined capacity of President of China, Chairman of the Chinese Communist Party, and Chairman of the Communist Party CMC.[96] In *Jiefangjun Bao*, articles have referred to the PLAN headquarters as the Navy's *tongshuaibu*, and to the CMC as the *tongshuaibu*.[97] Thus, while it is possible that the reference to a valid firing order means that it comes from the commander of the Second Artillery, the consensus among American scholars who follow the PLA closely is that in the context of nuclear and missile-firing orders, *tongshuaibu* refers to the CMC. This is the highest and most centralized level of military leadership in the Chinese Communist Party.[98] In the photo of Hu Jintao that appeared in *Jiefangjun Bao* depicting his 40th Anniversary speech to the leaders of the Second Artillery, Hu was wearing a PLA uniform without insignia or rank. Moreover, to confirm that the *tongshuaibu* is the CMC, in another account of Hu Jintao's speech published by *Xinhua News Service*, Hu is quoted as saying "The Second Artillery Corps is a strategic force directly commanded and used by the Party Central Committee and the CMC and is our core force for strategic deterrence."[99]

Second Artillery command orders are centralized, encoded and protected, and require human authentication. PLA military writers eschew completely automated command and control systems. There is a very strong emphasis on the need for a "man in the loop" even in modern, information age warfare. One writer specializing in command and control issues makes the point that "no matter how advanced a computer is used in a command and control system, it will never substitute for the strength and utility of the human brain."[100] The implications of this insistence on a "man in the loop" for nuclear firing orders is that the PLA will likely reject calls for automated protective action links in its doctrine.

Discussions about No First Use.

New interpretations of the concept of the "self-defensive counterattack" in the strategy of active defense and the general view that ballistic missiles are a kind of trump card in war bring into question whether the CMC will adhere to the stated "no-first-use" doctrine. Increasingly, China's military thinkers view missiles as a sort of "trump card" in war that will guarantee success for the PLA. Military thinkers are also very critical of the failure of Iraq's military to use ballistic missiles early, in mass, and effectively against the American and allied military build-up in the First Gulf War.

There is an open debate among civilian strategic thinkers, younger military officers, and the older leaders of the PLA on the utility of the "no-first-use" doctrine for China. This is important to follow because the CMC of the Chinese Communist Party ultimately has the finger on China's nuclear trigger, and technologically oriented civilians today, not former leaders of the PLA, control the CMC.

This leads to some doubt over whether its pledges would survive a deep crisis or conventional conflict. As discussed earlier in this paper, there is some ambiguity over what type of warheads ballistic missiles used to attack deployed naval battle groups would carry. Moreover, as discussed earlier in this paper, *China's National Defense in 2006* does not settle the ambiguity over how the CMC might make its decisions on what weapons to employ. There is also ambiguity over how China might respond to intelligence warnings of attack, and how China would respond to a conventional attack on its strategic systems.

According to a university based professor, an expert on arms control and disarmament often consulted by the PLA, it was he who suggested to PLA and central government policy planners that China should consider a nuclear response if its strategic systems were attacked, even if that attack was by conventional means.[101] Both the PLA and central government policy planners were cool to this idea, the professor said. Indeed, senior military officers and diplomats insisted that China must strictly abide by its "no first use" pledge. Nonetheless, the professor continues to push the discussion, often supported by younger scholars and military officers. The subject is not closed, and policy could shift with leadership generations.

The campaign theory text by Xue Xinglin of the National Defense University is quite clear on the matter of China's "no first use" policy. Xue writes that "the PRC will conduct a nuclear counterattack only after the enemy carries out a nuclear surprise attack."[102] Another seminal PLA text, for which former Chief of the General Staff Department General Zhang Wannian is credited as the editor, also makes explicit statements that the PLA will not initiate the use of nuclear weapons in war: "China's nuclear force is a self-defensive force. It is designed to protect the nation and deter nuclear attack."[103]

Zhang Wannian's explicit declaration echoes statements in an earlier book by Lu Hui, a long-time PLA expert on nuclear, chemical, and biological weapons. Lu explains that the genesis of China's own nuclear program was nuclear threats by the United States in the Korean War. The objective of becoming a nuclear power was "breaking the United States and Soviet great power monopoly on nuclear weapons."[104] Former defense minister and head of China's nuclear program General Zhang Aiping and the former head of the PLA National Defense University General Zhang Zhen endorse Lu's book as authoritative.

Lu quotes a Japanese scholar to make the point that one reason that China developed nuclear weapons was so that "the world will note China's latent power."[105] Lu reiterates that China's goal in developing nuclear weapons is to "break the monopoly of big nuclear powers and their nuclear threat, but that at no time and under no circumstances will China be the first to use nuclear weapons—China will be a completely independent state with nuclear weapons."[106] This position accurately reflects the policies announced by China's senior leaders on a number of occasions.

Despite these statements of doctrine, there are indications of dissent by junior officers. In a discussion analyzing the First Gulf War, Xin Qin notes that despite an advantage in ballistic missiles, Iraq's forces never used them effectively. Xin argues that had Iraqi forces massed their ballistic missile fires early against a weaker coalition that was just in the build-phase of its deployment, they could have had a deadly effect. By waiting for coalition forces to fully deploy, train and disperse into combat formations, Iraqi forces missed the opportunity to destroy the coalition before they moved into combat. Xin's conclusion is that Iraq did not act decisively with initiative when it should have, and it did not mass its fires for deadly effect.[107] All of this suggests that consideration be given to preemptive action, especially using ballistic missiles, when enemy intentions become clear, even if no attack has taken place.

Xin goes on to argue that "when one is fighting an enemy that fears heavy military casualties, one can attack major enemy political, military, and economic objectives in the enemy homeland and wipe out his massed forces."[108] Such a form of war can become a "war without engagement" because it uses long-range weapons and massed fires to wipe out the enemy's combat capability. Later in the same book, however, Xin makes the argument that "guided missiles are limited tools in warfare. They have to be used only against high value targets because their greatest worth is as a deterrent tool. Thus, guided missiles are 'political weapons' that have a political effect on a war."[109] The final argument on the uses of missiles in war by Xin is that missiles are weapons of choice to seize the initiative in combat and regain the offensive.[110]

Xin Qin is probably representative of a number of younger PLA officers that are not committed by virtue of long ideological education to the no first use of nuclear weapons policy. Clearly, he and other junior officers see the utility of preemption and the utility of the first use of these weapons, if the calculus can come out on China's side and massive nuclear retaliation can be avoided. Also, there is some ambiguity between the use of missiles and nuclear weapons at the campaign level and at the strategic level of war, but these younger officers do not dismiss using them out of hand.

There is wide acceptance of the doctrine of no first use at all levels of the PLA. Nonetheless, it is also apparent that nuclear strategists chafe at the doctrine and younger strategists, in particular, leave open in their writings the possibility that China may have to move away from this doctrine. Certainly at the theater level, the PLA leaves itself room to preempt an attack, even with nuclear weapons, if they believe this is a "nuclear counterattack" on an enemy about to launch a nuclear strike.

Conclusions.

Examining the doctrinal text, *Zhanyi Lilun Xuexi Zhinan (A Guide to the Study of Campaign Theory)* provided more information on China's nuclear doctrine, force deployment, command and control, and survivability measures than has been available in the past. Combining the examination of authoritative doctrinal text with materials from the Chinese press and those obtained through the Open Source Center helped to confirm the authenticity of the doctrinal text and provided supporting evidence for judgments about the nature of China's strategic rocket forces, their organization, readiness levels, and their control.

Another critical factor in the nuclear threat equation faced in the United States is the calculation by the CMC that China is able to absorb nuclear strikes with less catastrophic effects that the United States. This judgment is a function of China's historical military culture, geography, and an intentional state-directed policy of civil defense and risk distribution.[111] For the United States, this means that Chinese leaders may miscalculate American will and mistakenly take risky actions.

The decision by Beijing to put nuclear and conventional warheads on the same classes of ballistic missiles and colocate them near each other in firing units of the Second Artillery Corps also increases the risk of accidental nuclear conflict. If a country with good surveillance systems, like the United States, detects a missile being launched, it has serious choices to make. It can absorb a first strike, see whether it is hit with a nuclear or conventional weapon, and retaliate in kind; or it can decide to launch a major strike on warning. If the nation under attack has ballistic missile defenses, it might be able to stop an incoming missile and seek other ways to reduce tensions and a wide war.

A critical factor in any American decision will be the capabilities of American space-based sensor systems. Accurate sensors may be able to determine whether China launched a conventional or nuclear-tipped missile, and such a determination could prevent immediate escalation of a crisis or conflict.

However, some PLA officers advocate the capability for China to ensure that foreign surveillance assets cannot observe China from space. Indeed, on two occasions in recent months, the PLA has taken actions to demonstrate that it has moved from theoretical research and simulations of space warfare to demonstrate the capability to blind or destroy satellites over China. Moreover, the commander of the Second Artillery Corps has postponed a visit to the United States Strategic Command (STRATCOM) at the invitation of the STRATCOM commander, to engage in a strategic dialogue about such matters as a means of threat reduction.

The discussion of the need to mass missile fire and use missiles decisively, with surprise, in a theater war also undermines the likelihood that China would adhere to its own declared "no first use" policy. These considerations also reinforce the need for the United States to have effective ballistic missile defenses.

Perhaps the most serious questions raised in this paper are about the PLA's concentrated efforts to attack a deployed, moving aircraft carrier battle group. The PLA is coming closer to achieving that capability. The ambiguity over what form any ballistic (or cruise) missile attack might take creates a volatile situation in case of any crisis over Taiwan, or between China and Japan.

Finally, the debate inside China over the viability of its "no first use" policy is real. At present, older veterans of the Foreign Ministry and the PLA insist that the policy stay unchanged. However, younger scholars, soldiers, and diplomats will keep up the pressure to pull back from this policy, which requires continued attention and strategic dialogue with China's policy community.

At present, China has no real-time global space surveillance capability. Therefore, warning of impending nuclear attack must come from human intelligence. A global surveillance capability requires a system of relay satellites, which China is building but has not achieved. Thus, as China's space surveillance improves over the next decade, its nuclear doctrine will probably evolve.

These are serious matters for the American armed forces. China's nuclear forces are evolving and the way they are used is under debate. The way that the PLA handles its commitment to dominating space and its commitment to being capable of attacking American C4ISR systems affects strategic warning, missile defenses, and command and control. For the Army, with the responsibility to defend the United States against missile attack, it means that watching the evolution of this debate in China is critical to success.

ENDNOTES

1. Xue Xinglin, *Zhanyi Lilun Xuexi Zhinan (A Guide to the Study of Campaign Theory)*, Beijing: National Defense University Press, 2002.

2. Wang Houqing and Zhang Xingye, *et al.*, *Zhanyi Xue (The Science of Campaigns)*, Beijing: National Defense University Press, 2000. *Zhanyi Xue* is an "internal distribution only" (restricted, or *neibu*) PLA book, although a number of copies have made it into the United States and are circulating in academic and policy circles. *Zhanyi Lilun Zhinan* is available in PLA bookstores and explains many of the concepts in the restricted volume.

3. Sun Yiming and Yang Liping, *Xinxihua Zhanzheng Zhong de Zhanshhu Shuju Lian (Tactical Data Links in Information Warfare)*, Beijing: Beijing Post and Telecommunications College Press, 2005, pp. 5, 276-314.

4. This 1999 book set out the major tasks for future military development by the PLA. It has an effect on military development analogous to the *Quadrennial Defense Review* in the United States, setting major defense goals and time lines to accomplish them. It is important because, in large measure, the PLA has been successful in achieving these goals. Zhang Wannian, Ed. *Dangdai Shijie Junshi yu Zhongguo Guofang (China's National Defense and Contemporary World Military Affairs)*, Beijing: Military Science Press, 1999.

5. Hong Kong *Cheng Ming,* in Foreign Broadcast Information Service (FBIS) Open Source Center CPP20060714715009, July 13, 2006, *www.opensource.gov*. *Cheng Ming* has served as an outlet for information released by the Chinese Communist Party for decades, although it is a private magazine that is not owned by the PRC government.

6. Wang Zhongquan, *Meiguo He Liliang yu He Zhanlue (American Nuclear [Weapons] Strength and Nuclear Strategy)*, Beijing: National Defense University Press, 1995, pp. 125-126.

7. Yun Shan, "Zhimian Xin Junshi" (Facing New Military Transformation Squarely), *Liaowang Xinwen Zhoukan (Clear Lookout News Weekly)*, No. 28, July 14, 2003, p. 20.

8. Xin Qin, *Xinxihua Shidai de Zhanzheng (Warfare in the Information Age)*, Beijing: National Defense University Press, 2000, pp. 297-299. The use of missiles as "trump cards" or magic, "assassin's mace" weapons *(sa shou jian)* to win a war is discussed in Ge Xinliu, Mao Guanghong, and Yu Bo, "Xinxi Zhan zong de Daodan Budui Mianlin de Wenti yu Duice" (The Problems Faced by Guided Missile Forces in Information Warfare and Countermeasures), in Guofangdaxue Bianjibu, *Wo Jun Xinxizhan Wenti Yanjiu (Research on Information Warfare Problems for the PLA)*, Beijing: NDU Press, 1999, pp. 188-192. The latter book is a closely held compilation of papers for PLA internal use only from a PLA-wide conference on information warfare.

9. Zhang Wannian, ed., *Dangdai Shijie Junshi yu Zhongguo Guofang (China's National Defense and Contemporary World Military Affairs)*, Beijing: Military Science Press, 1999, p. 107-108. Although the book is 7 years old, it is perhaps the most authoritative statement of China's defense posture published by the PLA in a decade. It stands like a future defense posture statement for the PLA and contains guidance for military doctrine and acquisition, much of which has been accomplished in the years since it was published.

10. *Ibid.*, p. 202.

11. *Ibid.*

12. Xia Liping, "China's Military Strategy of Active Defense," *Xuexi Shibao*, December 12, 2005, in Open Source Center, CPP2005122325001, *www.opensource.gov*.

13. Li Jijun, *Junshi Zhanlue Siwei (Thinking about Military Strategy)*, Beijing: Military Science Press, 1996, 2000, 2002, pp. 188-189.

14. China's security thinkers do not ignore other powerful states like Japan, India, and Russia, but they see the United States as the greatest potent threat. A good example of how other powerful states are treated is Wang Yizhou, *Dangdai Guoji ZhengzhiBanlun (A Review of Contemporary International Politics)*, Shanghai:

Shanghai People's Press, 1995. Wang, a senior researcher with the Chinese Academy of Social Sciences, identified a range of potential security threats to China. Wang sees China's security environment as a complicated mix of old and new security threats. Some of these are clear, and some latent. Russia is a former threat and is now too weak militarily to be a major threat to China. In addition, Russia's security cooperation and arms sales to China make it a significantly lower threat than was the Soviet Union. India's growing nuclear capacity is a latent threat, while Pakistan is seen as a threat only if it becomes a radical Islamic state. Wang sees Japan as a clear potential threat to China because of its modern, strong air force and navy, its alliance with the United States, and its history of aggression. The clearest threat, however, although it is a "potential or latent threat," is the United States. Moreover, American security policies such as the emphasis on expanding democracy and the fact that the United States is the sole world superpower capable of coercing other nations, make it the greatest potential strategic threat to China for both political and military reasons.

15. Li, *Junshi Zhanlue Siwei*, pp. 210-212.

16. Yan Xuetong, ed., *Zhongguo Guojia Liyi Fenxi (An Analysis of China's National Interest)*, Tianjin: Tianjin People's Press, 1997, p. 158. Senior scholars at the American Studies Center of Fudan Univeristy in Shanghai also acknowledge the United States as a major power whose military capabilities alone can threaten China. Meeting at Fudan University, June 24, 2006.

17. Information Office of the People's Republic of China State Council, *China's National Defense in 2006,* December 2006. In Open Source Center, 0630 GMT, December 29, 2006, FEA20061230063508.

18. Xia, "China's Military Strategy of Active Defense."

19. See Andrew Scobell, *China's Use of Military Force: Beyond the Great Wall and the Long March*, New York: Cambridge University Press, 2003, pp. 34-35.

20. *Ibid.*, p. 35. Scobell quotes Marshall Peng Dehuai and other PLA researchers from the Academy of Military Science in his discussion of the active defense.

21. Discussions with scholars in Shanghai and Beijing, June 2006.

22. There are two types of missile campaigns: the nuclear counterattack campaign and the conventional guided missile attack campaign. The latter (conventional) involves surprise and sudden, preemptive action, Xue, p. 148. Two points in contemporary PLA doctrine are relevant here. The first emphasizes that "in modern warfare the application of firepower involves the use of precision guided missiles," and the second that "sudden attacks and surprise attacks are the route to success in warfare." See Li Bingyan, *Da Moulue yu Xin Junshi Biange (Grand Strategy and the New Revolution in Military Affairs)*, Beijing: Military Science Press, 2004, pp. 52, 56.

23. Xue, p. 393.

24. *Ibid.*, p. 394.

25. *Ibid.*, pp. 393-394.

26. *Ibid.*, p. 153.

27. Zhang Wannian, ed., *Dangdai Shijie Junshi yu Zhongguo Guofang* (China's National Defense and Contemporary World Military Affairs), Beijing: Military Science Press, 1999, p. 114.

28. Xin, pp. 298-299.

29. *Ibid.*, pp. 94-95.

30. The author was a military attaché in China between 1988 and 1990 and from 1995 to the end of 1997. In the intervening years, the author visited China regularly as a strategist on the Army staff and met with PLA officers and senior military delegations. This paragraph summarizes their comments.

31. Xue, pp. 384-400.

32. Xin, p. 88.

33. *Ibid.*, pp. 88-89.

34. Liu Mingtao, Yang Chengjun, *et al.*, eds., *Gao Jishu Zhanzheng Zhong de Daodan Zhan (Ballistic Missile Battles in High Technology Warfare)*, Beijing: National Defense University Press, 1993, p. 15.

35. *Ibid.*, p. 11.

36. *Ibid.*

37. DF stands for *Dong Feng*, which means "East Wind."

38. Guo Wujun, *Lun Zhanlue Zhihui (On Strategic Command and Control)*, Beijing: Military Science Press, 2001, p. 226.

39. Nie Yubao, "Daji haishang di da jian jianting biandui de dianzi zhan zhanfa" (Combat Methods for Electronic Warfare Attacks on Heavily Fortified Enemy Naval Formations), in Military Science Editorial Group, *Wo Jun Xixi Zhan Wenti Yanjiu (Research on Questions about Information Warfare in the PLA)*, Beijing: National Defense University Press, 1999, pp. 183-187.

40. *Ibid*.

41. Ge Xinliu, Mao Guanghong, and Yu Bo, "Xinxi zhan zhong daodan budui mianlin de wenti yu duici," (Problems Faced by Guided Missile Forces in Information Warfare Conditions and Their Countermeasures), in Military Science Editorial Group, *Wo Jun Xixi Zhan Wenti Yanjiu*, pp. 188-189.

42. Min Zengfu, *Kongjun Junshi Sixiang Gailun (An outline of Air Force Military Thought)*, Beijing: PLA Press, 2006, pp. 377-378.

43. Tan Shoulin and Zhang Daqiao, "Effective Range for Terminal Guidance Ballistic Missile Attacking Aircraft Carrier," in *Qingbao Zhihui Kongzhi yu Fangzhen Jishu (Information Command and Control Systems and Simulation Technology)*, Vol. 28, No. 4, August 2006, pp. 6-9.

44. *Ibid*. p. 9.

45. Li Xinqi, Tan Shoulin, and Li Hongxia, "Precaution Model Simulation Actualization on Threat of Maneuver Target Group at Sea," in *Qingbao Zhihui Kongzhi yu Fangzhen Jishu (Information Command and Control Systems and Simulation Technology)*, August 2005. In Opensource Center, November 25, 2005.

46. Xue, pp. 387-388.

47. The Central Military Commission's confidence that it will get advance warning of an attack has serious counterintelligence implications for the United States. At present, the PLA lacks a real-time, national technical collection capability. It will probably take at least 5 years for China to deploy sufficient real-time global surveillance assets. The PLA's confidence, therefore, implies that it has sufficient human intelligence assets in place in the United States to provide such warning.

48. Scobell, *China's Use of Military Force*, pp. 34-35.

49. Ge Xinliu, *et al.*, "Xinxi Zhan zhong daodan budui mianlin de wenti yu duice," (The Real Problems in Information War Encountered by Guided Missile Forces), Military Science Editorial Group, *Wo Jun Xixi Zhan Wenti Yanjiu (Research on Questions*

about Information Warfare in the PLA), Beijing: National Defense University Press, 1999, p. 189.

50. Pan Youmu, "Zhuoyan kongtian—ti hua tan suo kongtian anquan zhanlue" (Focus on Air–Space Integration and Study National Air–Space Security Strategy), *Zhongguo Junshi Kexue (China Military Science)*, Beijing: Vol. 19, February 2006, pp. 60-66; quote from p. 66.

51. Wendell Minnick, "China Flexes Space Muscles: Satellite Destruction Highlights Beijing's Focus," *Defense News*, January 22, 2007, p. 7.

52. Xue, pp. 148-153.

53. Xia Liping, "China's Military Strategy of Active Defense," *Xuexi Shibao*, December 12, 2005, in Open Source Center, CPP2005122325001, *www.opensource.gov*.

54. *Ibid.* See also Xue, p. 384.

55. Xue, p. 267. See also Zhang Wannian, ed., *Dangdai Shijie Junshi yu Zhongguo Guofang (China's National Defense and Contemporary World Military Affairs)*, Beijing: Military Science Press, 2000, p. 202.

56. Xue, p. 385.

57. *Ibid.*

58. *Ibid.*, p. 384.

59. *Ibid.* According to the International Institute for Strategic Studies (IISS), the PLAAF has one nuclear-ready regiment of up to 20 H-6 (Tu-16) *Badger* bombers on standby. See IISS, *The Military Balance 2006*, London: Routledge, 2006, p. 268.

60. Peng Guangqian and Yao Youzhi, *The Science of Military Strategy.* Beijing: Military Science Publishing House, 2005, p. 218. This is the English language translation, with some updates, of Peng Guangqian, *et al.*, eds., *Zhanlue Xue 2001 (On Strategy 2001)*, Beijing: Military Science Press, 2001.

61. *Ibid.*

62. On this doctrine, see Cheng Feng and Larry M. Wortzel, "PLA Operational Principles and Limited War; The Sino-Indian War of 1962," in Mark A. Ryan, David M. Finklestein, and Michael McDevitt, eds., *Chinese Warfighting: The PLA Experience Since 1949*, Armonk, NY: M. E. Sharpe, 2003, pp. 180-183, 194-195.

63. Xin Qin reinforces this, writing that "one must attack the C4ISR network that supports the command and control system of an enemy, particularly one that is fighting a war on external lines (in other words, an enemy fighting a power projection war)," Xin, p. 90.

64. *Ibid.*, pp. 384-385. These targeting priorities are repeated in a basic level PLA publication intended to educate the average soldier or junior officer on modern, high technology in war. This book says that nuclear-tipped intercontinental ballistic missiles target enemy political and economic centers, military bases, important defense industrial base areas, nuclear weapons storage depots, key communications hubs, and other such strategic targets. See Guo Yanhua, *et al.*, eds., *Jushi Jishu Aomi Jieyi (Explaining the "Mysteries" of Military High Technology)*, Beijing: National Defense University Press, 2005, p. 123.

65. Xue, p. 385. See also Liu Mingtao, Yang Chengjun, *et al*, eds. *Gao Jishu Zhanzheng Zhong de Daodan Zhan (Ballistic Missile Battles in High Technology Warfare)*, Beijing: National Defense University Press, 1993, p. 116. Ge Xinliu, Mao Guanghong and Yu Bo, *Wo Jun Xinxizhan Wenti Yanjiu (PLA Research on Problems of Information Warfare)*, Beijing: NDU Press, 1999, pp. 188-192.

66. *Ibid.*, p. 387.

67. *Ibid.*, p. 388.

68. U.S. Defense Threat Reduction Agency, Conference Report: U.S.-China Strategic Dialogue, Honolulu, HI, August 1-3, 2005, Executive Summary, p. 1.

69. *Ibid.*

70. "Second Artillery Force Communications Regiment Drills Hard to Achieve Proficiency in Communication Skills," *Jiefangjin Bao*, February 16, 2006, *www.jiefangjunbao.com.cn*, in Open Source Center CPP20060216502004.

71. Xue, pp. 153, 390-391, 394.

72. Xin, p. 16.

73. Xue, p. 387.

74. *Ibid.*, pp. 387-388.

75. *Ibid.*, p. 389.

76. *Ibid.*

77. *Ibid.*, p. 391.

78. *Ibid.*

79. *Ibid.*, p. 153.

80. *Ibid.*, p. 390.

81. *Ibid.*

82. FBIS Open Source Center, *rccb.osis.gov*, June 29, 2006, 2:27 PM.

83. Zhang Junkong and Wang Qingyong, "Research Results of Combat food Supply by a Second Artillery Base Fills the Gap," *Beijing Huojianbing Bao,* November 26, 2005, p. 1, in FBIS Open Source Center CPP20051227318002.

84. Tang Xudong, "Happy To Be the Safety Fuse in the Transport of National Treasure," *Huojianbiing Bao,* November 3, 2005, p. 2, in Open Source Center CPP20051227318011.

85. Zhang Ligang and Kang Fushun, "Trans-Regional Mobile Training Becomes Booster of Combat Capabilities," *Huojianbing Bao,* June 13, 2006, p. 1, in Open Source Center CPP2006 0710318004.

86. "Second Artillery Paper Reports Debates over 'Prestigious' Missile Position Design," *Huojianbing Bao,* April 1, 2006, p. 2, in Open Source Center CPP20060901318003.

87. Xue, p. 387.

88. *Ibid.*

89. *Ibid.*, p. 392.

90. See Huang Luwei, Bi Yiming, and Yang Yifeng, "Research on Missile Forces Network Centric Warfare," in *Zhihui Kongzhi yu Fanghen (Command, Control and Simulation),* April 1, 2006, pp. 18-21, in Open Source Center CPP200609077476001.

91. Liu and Yang, *Gao Jishu Zhanzheng Zhong de Daodan Zhan*, p. 107.

92. *Ibid.*, p. 108.

93. Xue, p. 386.

94. Wang Zhongquan, *Meiguo He Liliang yu He Zhanlue*, pp. 69-74.

95. *Ibid.*, 388.

96. *Jiefangjun Bao,* June 30, 2006, p. 1, FBIS Open Source Center CPP20060630718002.

97. See *www.chinamil.com.cn/jbzlk/outline/Jiefangjun Bao,* April 21, 2006, and May 25, 2006.

98. See Michael S. Chase and Evan Medieros, "China's Evolving Calculus: Modernization and Doctrinal Debate," in James Mulvenon and David Finklestein, *China's Revolution in Doctrinal Affairs: Emerging Trends in the Operational Art of the Chinese People's Liberation Army,* Arlington, VA: Rand Corporation and the Center for Naval Analysis, 2006, p. 147; Ken Allen and Maryanne Kivlehan-Wise, Implementing PLA Second Artillery Doctrinal Reforms, in Mulvenon and Finklestein, *China's Revolution in Doctrinal Affairs,* pp. 159-200; and Bates Gill, James Mulvenon, and Mark Stokes, "The Chinese Second Artillery Corps: Transition to Credible Deterrence," in James Mulvenon and Andrew N. D. Yang, eds., *The People's Liberation Army as an Organization*, Santa Monica, CA: Rand Corporation, 2002, pp. 510-586. The author is also grateful to M. Scot Tanner of the Rand Corporation and David Cowhig of the U.S. Department of State for their insights on the term as it is used by the Second Artillery.

99. *Xinhua News Service,* July 2, 2005, in FBIS Open Source Center, "Account of Party Central Committee's Care and Concern for Strategic Missile Units," *rccb.osis.gov,* July 5, 2006, 12:30 AM.

100. Xin, p. 16.

101. Interview in China with the professor by the author, June 2006.

102. Xue, p. 385.

103. Zhang, *Dangdai Shijie Junshi yu Zhongguo Guofang*, p. 203.

104. Lu Hui, ed., *HeHuaSheng Wuqi de Lishi yu Welai (The History of Nuclear, Chemical and Biological Weapons and their Future)*, Beijing: Military Science Press, 1991, p. 103.

105. *Ibid.*, p. 127.

106. *Ibid.*, p. 132.

107. Xin, pp. 88-89.

108. *Ibid.*, p. 90.

109. *Ibid.*, p. 297.

110. *Ibid.*, p. 299.

111. The level of tolerance for the risk of nuclear war is explored in Xiao Xingbo, *He Zhanzheng yu Renfang (People's Air*

Defense and Nuclear War), Beijing: People's Liberation Army Press, 1989. This is a book "for internal distribution only." The questions of preparations, civil defense and nuclear calculus can also be found in Zhu Mingquan *He Kuosan: Weixian yu Fangzhi (Nuclear Proliferation: Danger and Prevention),* Shanghai Science and Technology Literature Press, 1995; and Yao Yunzhu, *Zhanhou Meiguo Weishe Lilun yu Zhengce (Post-War American Deterrence Theories and Policies)*, Beijing: National Defense University Press, 1998.

CPSIA information can be obtained at www.ICGtesting.com
Printed in the USA
LVOW05s0900120614

389749LV00005B/106/P